Patient Wait

by

Rachel Michelle Schroeder

Cover

Illustrated by Winter Rose Lynne Waple

"Dad's Poems"

by

Paul Michael Schroeder

1951-2024

rachelmichelle@patientwaitbook.com

www.patientwaitbook.com

Copyright © 2025 Patient Wait Book

All Rights Reserved

Within the pages of this book are many of the emotions we, as human beings, are capable of feeling. Most of us anyhow. Within any writing is the ability to use one's own perception to create a narrative that correlates with our own experiences. This is one of the beautiful things about words, while also the most dangerous.

This book is dedicated to all of those out there like me. Imperfect with a little crazy. Compassionate and strong. I have not always made the right choices. And, sometimes, it took more than once for me to learn my lesson. After the storms and darkness, I can still smile. I have been weakened and controlled by my heart which led to painful lessons. I have broken other's hearts which also led to painful lessons. I have stayed when I should have walked away, and I have walked away when I should have stayed. Wrong place at the wrong time. Right place at the right time. Blessed. Humbled.

For everything, I am thankful. I am still here. I am unapologetically who I am. God's child.

To my children- YOU ARE MY EVERYTHING. I love you... across the universe.

Dad- This is for YOU! You were my mentor and, in my eyes, the greatest writer in the world! I hope I have made you proud. So much.

J- Death does not stop love. It does not stop the heart from beating. It does not miraculously stop feelings. I miss you every single day. You will always be my love.

TABLE OF CONTENTS

DADS POEMS: The Wolf and the Rabbit and Believe Again

1. Darkness Control
2. lost within (formerly Unforgiven)
3. Broke Down
4. Dead Fate
5. Always Say I Love You
6. Her Tears
7. Replaced
8. On This Day
9. My Reasons
10. Meaning What
11. Only a Human Being
12. WRONG
13. "Not You"
14. STOLEN Pleasure
15. Mama Knows Best
16. Screams
17. There he Stood
18. waves
19. YOU KNEW
20. What more do you want from me
21. Unprepared
22. I Don't Like Her
23. See Me Again
24. Her Perfect World
25. God
26. Having a child in a nutshell

27. A Myth
28. This White Rose
29. Damn It Man
30. redemption
31. Mislead
32. White Flag
33. open door
34. Who Knows Better
35. My Love
36. it is you
37. FEAR
38. Notice Me
39. February
40. reuniting
41. Not Over Yet
42. Pissed Off
43. The Hardest
44. Story Book: Chapter One
45. Story Book: Chapter Two
46. Story Book: Chapter Three
47. Story Book: Chapter Four
48. Gold Specs
49. Impossible Vengeance
50. Silent Noise
51. It's a Thin Line
52. Silly Boy
53. This Battle
54. The Difference
55. you're a fool
56. An Innocent Heart
57. Was it You?

58. Sleepless Minutes
59. Nothing to Say
60. touched by an angel
61. This Pain
62. Stay Calm
63. I Question You This
64. Walk Away
65. Nothing you can buy me
66. Scattered
67. Stolen Again
68. Trust
69. J
70. I Gave In
71. it is in a name
72. WHAT I GET
73. No Worries (2)
74. This Night
75. Skin Deep
76. the battle between myself and I
77. A Special Thank You
78. I Am Bound
79. Shed No Tears
80. Predicament
81. Karma Past
82. Karma Present
83. Roses Burst Into Flames
84. October
85. I Will See You There
86. This is me
87. Gone
88. Think Before You Act

89. Smiling
90. They fucking lied
91. The Exact Thing
92. hurt me if you will
93. do not stop
94. Words
95. Take A Bow
96. With Me
97. A Reason
98. You Made Me Do This
99. Trust Your Heart
100. Well?!?
101. NO
102. permission
103. Fresh Pain
104. Opposites
105. Haylee
106. versus
107. Contradictory
108. Hard to Follow
109. Sweet Darkness
110. Lesson Learned
111. Nothing But a Dream
112. Prisoner
113. Recurring Moments
114. Scarred For Life
115. Trying Too Hard
116. Wake Up
117. I Evoke You
118. Wish and Burn
119. You Tell Me

120. Who I am vs Who I Can Be: Part I
121. Who I am vs Who I Can Be: Part II

believe again

My daughter gave me a chair
It was broken
And my spirit was broken as we
To Hell I had been
In between spurts
Of energy erupting
Within my soul.
"No More" has been long-forgot
As a worm I learned to live
Again and again, MRS Then a
I see the route I've been.
To be free

16/8/2008

The Wolf and the Rabbit
Once played
But!
Together their paths were misplaced
Upon crossing the circle
Confusion grew.

The spirit within them
Flew
Askew to the whim of the wind
Crossing one another
And, for the last time, Mrs Thomas
Sent the rabbit and Wolf
Into scenes unknown
And! Not desired to be viewed.

The Wolf and the Rabbit
No longer are allowed to play
But, in time
Together their paths will realign
Into crossing the circle again
Confusion brew.
Allready!

pms

Darkness Control

There was nothing left to do but watch
As the night faded for the last time into the dawn
There were no reasons left behind
As to why the sun no longer shined
There were no choices to be made
As they were made before the sun had a say
There were no reasons to wait any longer
The darkness had already had its chance to take over
There was not enough time to notice
The eternal mistake the night had made
For all the innocence the sun once saved
Slowly died and decayed away

Lost Within
(Formerly Unforgiven)

As I sit and watch the rain
I wonder hopeless thoughts of underserving pain
I turn to look
You are never there
When I need you the most
You're the farthest away
You're not doing your deed
Of fulfilling my dreams
My heart has been breaking
My tears start to fall
My thoughts won't stop
My wounds won't heal
You promised me the world
And delivered me Hell
Along with my love I gave you my life
My heart and my soul
Engraved with your lies
The memory destroys me more every day
The bleeding inside you left behind
I will always remember you for one thing
Leading me into this darkness I am still lost within

Broke Down

You broke me down and left me to deteriorate
Piece by piece you peel back the memories
Like vultures feeding off my skin
All that is left of this body
Is what you hesitated to destroy
Just who do you think you are?
To steal my dreams and mutilate my heart?
No more nights lying there waiting
The years of pain have been replaced
Now the only question remaining
Should I do to you what you've done to me?
Shattered my soul and crumbled my dreams
I have no choice but to leave
I am not dying or breathing
I am just watching and waiting
Someday, someway, someone will give you what you deserve

Dead Fate

You'll dream of me tonight
You'll awake to the morning light
I'll run through your mind... one more time
But it's too late, I don't think I can wait
For you to come around, stop being so scared
I might be wrong again
I think maybe fate could win
So, I guess you may be right
Dreaming could be useless
It could take our fate and kill it

I dreamt of you last night
And in the morning light
You disappeared without warning
You never ran through my mind again
It is too late, I could not wait
You never came around, why were you so scared?
I was wrong again
I thought fate could win
So, I guess you're definitely right
Dreaming is useless
Right in front of my face
It took my fate and killed it

Always Say I Love You

Has anyone ever told you
in a hypnotic way
How much they love you
How much you mean
Have you ever turned
Because of selfish needs
On someone who cares
Someone who means well
Has anyone ever hurt you
In ways you cannot explain
Or pretended not to notice
They were too busy with themselves
Has anyone ever told you
Trying to protect your heart
They have no pain lingering
Because you're the one behind it
Has anyone ever pushed you away
With no warning or no reason
Leaving you to wonder forever
What the Hell you did
Have you forgotten
The last words you spoke
And without even considering
There would never be another chance to remember

Her Tears

The tears she cries tonight are not for you,
And the ache in her heart has been there before.
She watched her life fall to the ground,
A thousand times over she has felt the pain.
She climbs the tallest mountain she can find,
Falling to her knees, she's gone too far.
She cries out for someone to hear her… if you listen.

Is there anyone out there just like me?
Is this an impossible dream?
Is there anyone out there who could understand?
Just like me…is this an impossible dream?

The daylight shined on the darkest morning,
I guess there was no one to hear her (again).
She waited until the last possible moment,
A thousand times over she has felt the fear.
She climbed the tallest mountain she could find,
Falling to her knees, she took her life.
Still to this day, you can hear her cries…

If you listen.

Replaced?

The sun burned me again today, because your love, it took away

The tragic beliefs I am finding dead, the night came with no defense

Don't leave me here forever, don't leave me here to wonder

Don't leave me here to desire, don't leave me here to remember

Don't leave me here with this pain…

Don't leave me here to die again.

On This Day

On this day I give you my hand

On this day you give me your last name

Get ready, because it's forever now

Come Hell or high water, it's you and I together

At times it is a terrifying thought

But in the end its all that mattered

There is a foundation as strong as ever

That we built this dream upon

And now our reality has been realized

It's everything I've ever wanted and more

Even after all of these years

The struggles, the tears, the smiles

And the unforgettable memories

Untouchable love united with three reasons to live

The flaws make it a perfect connection

I could live this life without you-

But it wouldn't be much of living

With you the sun shines through the rain

We have finally reached our destiny

My Reasons

Every time I watched her laugh
Every time he reached up to grab his brother's hand
When they fought amongst themselves
And I was ready to pull out my hair
Each time they tattled on each other
And I simply sighed and rolled my eyes
Each time we sat down for dinner together
And the sass I received for no electronics at the table
Every day I heard the best and worst part of their day
The foundation of memories that will last a lifetime
Every time he secretly mimicked his brothers' actions
The tears they held back at one another's accomplishments
How they would all start talking like the other through different phases
The ridiculous wrestling moves you only get away with, with a sibling
The mess left after a massive and unplanned food fight
Each time one would sneak up on and scare the Hell out of the other
The nights they all ended up in my bed because of thunder
Easing them after the upset of each game or debate lost
That terrifying silence when I knew they were up too no good
The way each of them had their own distinct way of communicating
The precise movements of placing an easter basket on the porch like a ninja
Every sleepless night wrapping presents in the dark undetected
Waiting for a call the first time they walked out that door alone
The handwritten names on the boxes sitting out in the garage
The Tupperware full of hand-made presents and school projects
The baby teeth hidden in the top drawer of my jewelry box
The beautiful smile my daughter wears
The contagious laugh my sons have
The way they protect one another
The way each has always done to the one after
The values each of them has infused in their subconscious
How proud I am of them could never be measured
I just can't believe when I see the transformations before me
They are the same little humans that used to need me for everything
And I still thank God every single day,
For blessing me with the three reasons I live

Meaning What

Life means nothing
We are all going to die
We put forth so much effort
Just to be shut down
After all our hard work
Things out of our control
Take our effort and our life
And shove it in the ground
We take ourselves up
Just to be shot down
We build this life
Just to be destroyed
Waiting for something
Never coming
No use in working so damn hard
No use in dreaming

Only a Human Being

And the emptiness takes over again
Trying to explain how I am feeling
It's an impossible feat
It's like a knife being twisted into your soul
Forgive me while I try to put it into words
Like your last breath
Your last heartbeat
The numbness is subtle as first
Your mind racing
A waterfall of tears builds
But, yet, do not fall
And then…. everything freezes in time
There's absolutely nothing
No thoughts, remember to breathe, disbelief
And when that moment comes
You realize your entire fucking world just imploded
Your future plans
Your twin flame
Only a human being

WRONG

i can't waLk again
i've drank too much again
where were you a mInute ago?
i couldn't find you
i looked in the bAthroom
i looked in the kitchen
the livingRoom was empty
the garage door is broken
a couple people chilL in the backyard
but no one was downstairs
i saw your car sittIng out front
but no one was in it
so where were you A minute ago?
I couldn't find you
why aRe you shaking?
are you cold?
where is the ring i gave you?
did you Leave it at home?
i'm starting to get nervous,
i really need to know
where were you a minute Ago?
were you not alone?
is theRe something you need to tell me?
something i might need to know?
you're shaking your head no…
but i feeL i'm being a fool
it's not that hard
i really need to know…
where were you a mInute ago?
what is thAt on your neck?
someone else's pair of lips??
i guess now i know…
i don't need to ask again…
where you were a minute ago…
is wheRe you should not have been!

"Not You"

You are scared
I have tried too hard
You live in fear
I live for the moment
You don't believe
In what we made
I can't adhere
My heart believes
I have tried too hard
To just let go
It won't let me
It's all you
I won't wait forever
Just for now
I can't turn away
I can't say goodbye
My heart believes
My mind follows
This is where I'm at
I'm coping

STOLEN Pleasure

Even as I scratched through his skin
He acted as if I wasn't there
Even though I am the one
He is tying to the floor
He is holding down with nothing
His eyes are full of emptiness
My muscles ache with torment
I can't pull myself back up
My back is broken and in pieces
My stomach is burning into my throat
ONLY once may it be taken
ONLY once may it be true
ONLY once to be concealed
ONLY once to be mistaken

ONLY once will you have this chance
Punishments are to be forsaken
Never again will you see
Into the eyes of another victim

His power and his strength
Aren't really there at all
It's just a mirror image
Of what he wished he'd become
Each time he took another's innocence
He turned into more of an empty soul
No remorse or lessons learned
What is this pain worth?
To kill is to save
To hurt is to wound
Once wounded forever
It can't be undone
Suffer in silence
As he did to you
Never remember what it felt like
To give the gift given to you
But instead, you get to remember
That gift you were given has been stolen

I better never see you again, I will return the pain

Mama Knows Best

Guess I should have listened mama

Guess I should have known better

Guess I should have taken your advice

Then maybe I guess I wouldn't be here

Guess I'll learn my lesson mama

Guess I'll have to wait a little longer

Guess my fate hasn't come for me yet

Then maybe I guess I'll have to keep waiting

Screams

All the words you did acclaim
Were nothing but a way to rid you of your pain
The distant yearn to grab ahold
The fading fight to keep control
Lifting me up to drown me out
Losing my love with no regrets
And now all that's left
Is the screaming silence that we made… tell me…
Can't you hear me in your dreams?
Can't you hear me through the screams?
When it seems, I can't go any farther
You find a way to make it harder
But I see inside, to where your selfishness hides
I see through…it really meant nothing to you
And for that, you can have your silence back
Never again… this lust is dead

There He Stood

I went walking by
There he stood
Passing him by
I then froze
His eyes locked on me
I turned away
His eyes looked through me
It seemed meant
He wanted me badly
I stood my ground
Later in the night
As we walked
Within my strength
I lost it all
He pulled me in
His kiss singed
His hands controlled
From the start
Pulling me closer
No room to breathe
He was danger
I still melted
That was then
This is now
Where he is
I do not know

Waves

I can feel this breaking through
Intensely pushing and pulling away
Only you could get me this high
No one has the desire I'm in need of
These standards of the normal ways
Pulling me lower and killing me slower
This feeling I can't seem to replace
Seemingly feeding off of my skin

Watching you fall back again
Remaining within the limited
Conquering all of my fear
An unimaginable circulation
No solution to turn back on
Distress isn't even a question
All is turned into pleasure
Look inside to find your answer

Once afraid and hiding away
Following my instincts again
Turning towards the inevitable
There you are not far behind me
Trying to grasp this sensitivity
Trying to endure and understand
Below a puddle of my tears
So offensive with such innocence

The sexual aroma is suffocating
Penetrating and the final destination
Kneeled over and impassive
Diminutive and analgesic sense of pain
Insensible to the torment
Without the loss of consciousness
The torture so invigorating
Persecuting gratification

YOU KNEW

I knew you wouldn't come through
But it doesn't matter
I still wait for the phone to ring
I still look everywhere for a sign
There is nothing lonelier than being alone
And I've been here for far too long

Why did you say you gave a damn?
When you knew it was a bold face lie.
Why did you make me stay?
When you knew you'd walk away.
Why?
Why?

I believed in what you said
But it doesn't matter
I still hold all these feelings back
I still want way more than I took
There is nothing more painful than a broken heart
And I've been patient for far too long

Why did you come at me like you did?
When you knew you had nothing to give.
Why did you say you cared at all?
When you knew you'd break my heart.
Why?
Why?

What More Do You Want From Me?

I pity your choices
I laugh at your pride
I tantalize your emotions
I drown out your fear
I break through your walls
I shower you with attention
I hold on to your fright
I wait for your affection
I feel the warmth of your skin
I watch you turn colder
I follow your lead
I lead your heart
I bury your past hurt
I burn your unwanted memories
I conquer your demons
I fight for your reasons
I lie for your strength
I cry for your reaction
I bring out your joy
I wallow in your pain

What more do you want from me?

Unprepared

I miss you everyday
I dream of the place
I wasn't ready for this change
I couldn't have prepared myself
This dying inside of me
When you had to leave
Though your legacy lives on
My life seems so empty
I still hold a grudge
Yes, I know it's not right

My heart cannot be complete
You're never coming back to me
There are no positive aspects to depend on
My power has grown unimaginably weak
The only true ending is so final in itself
Death came accordingly
In my soul, you're still breathing

Chills down my spine
Just one glimpse, just one time
Just one dream, if you could come to me
Just one moment of understanding
I know you're still watching over
But this nightmare never ends
I didn't have to chance to say anything
But your blood runs in my veins
Your pain ending and mine beginning
I couldn't choose it any other way
Though I would have taken your place
It wasn't my time yet

You're content-living after-no more pain

I Don't Like Her

When I'm with you I lose myself
I become someone that I'm not and I don't like her
And it's not you, it's me, it's where my mind goes
You used to bring out the good in me
But I feel that you haven't done that in so long
If I was there, it would be different, right?
I wouldn't go to those buried and at times dark places inside my mind
It's hard to find words, there are too many thoughts stirring
There are many things I want to say, some nice and sweet,
But others may be harsh and cut deep
But your words are so contradictory, so damn confusing
And you know I'm more of a straight shooter
So, I just don't do well with mind-fuckery
I'm truly sorry if me saying these things burn,
Trust me, it's not easy for me to feel this way
But it doesn't change the reality, that until I take back my heart
I will never be able to let someone else ignite it
And that's just not something I can keep wagering
We don't choose who we love,
But we choose if someone is worth losing or not.

See Me Again

I will wait for the day

I will wait patiently

I will wait to see if I see you again

Are you watching over me now?

Will you be there to take my hand?

Are you waiting to see me again?

Her Perfect World

She thinks she's perfect
Not a flaw
But reality is in question
It's coming hard
Watching in third person
Can't say a word
Because nobody knows anything
In her perfect world
She can't find her senses
They're too far gone
Lost in her own deception
She's falling hard
Who's going to help her
Out of her own cause
She doesn't realize
No one wants her to fall apart
She's got to listen someday
But she can't be ignored
She's going to have to manage
Her way out on her own
When blinded by your own confusion
Forever is even longer
When in the middle of a thousand bridges
And you've burnt them all
Inevitable choices for inevitable results

God

When I am ready to fold...

You lend me strength.

When I need to cry...

You lend me your tears.

When I fall to the ground...

You give me reason to rise.

When I think I've had enough of this life...

You show me how much I really have.

When my confidence gives out...

You make me see the beauty within.

When my dreams fall to pieces...

You make me believe what tomorrow can bring.

When I've lost all hope and all of my will...

You're the one that doesn't let me give in to the pain.

When the tears just won't stop,

When the days just won't end,

When the nightmares take over,

When I am fading into nonexistence.

When I just don't care to care anymore,

You're the one that is always there

For this I know... I will never be alone.

Having Children in a Nutshell

It all starts out as this...
The peace and quiet, the days of sleeping on your side and stomach
The excitement and nervousness, the announcement and congratulations
The nesting and organization, the house fully stocked, and laundry folded
The nausea and ridiculous cravings, the body pillow and sweat drenched blankets
The swollen feet and red leopard skin, the emotional distress and hormones igniting
The delirium and anticipation, the walking and intercourse to hurry it along
The prepping and taking inventory, the clock ticking and waiting forever

Then the sweet moment finally arrives...
The rush and one second of insanity, the intolerable pain and legit agony
The drugs and tears of happiness, the moment your life changes forever
The crying and screaming, the smiles and a million dirty diapers
The coos and crawling, the sleepless nights and spit up stained clothing
The first word and first laugh, the plastic plug ins and iced teething rings
The sweet smell and tiny toes, the gas drops and open mouth kisses
The first steps and forehead bruises, the chasing games and solid foods

Growing up...
The chicken pox and strep throat, the winter colds and summer flus
The antibiotics and allergy sprays, the dry fruity vitamins and itching cream
The bloody noses and deep cuts, the broken bones and first loves
The band-aids and self-adhesive gauze, the wrist splints and ER visits
The unmade bed and sticky floors, the smelly socks and Styrofoam cups
The real hugs and I love you's, the secret notes and rapid eyerolls.
The first car and first date, the sneaking out and failed attempts

Young adults...

The mistakes and midnight calls, the take-out dishes and empty toilet paper rolls
The "loaned" money and grocery runs, the tear-soaked shoulder and snotty tissues
The empty fridge and spaghetti rings, the pregnancy scares and hard learned lessons
The credit hours and work schedules, the keg parties and all-night cram sessions
The friendship and Sunday dinners, the conversations and meeting their partners
The celebrations and rites of passage, the self-reliance and building futures
The letting go and trusting God, the eternal love and the pride you hold

A Myth

True love is just a myth,

Friendship is just an excuse to get in

The sun outside is shining bright

But inside of me the storm has just began

I could use a drink to forget it all

Another one down, another memory revealed

There is no escape from the truth

Just like always, I will pretend I'm not hurting

It is not a longing, just like thunder rumbling within my heart

Being let down by the one I trusted most

The one that should have never hurt me

Is the one that has hurt me the most

The one I thought I could always trust

Betrayed deeper than anyone ever has done before

I held out my hand, just to be fooled

This White Rose

A strong heart behind the sorrow
A love that beats through the pain
Within the walls of the armor
A frightened woman stands

Full of love for all created
Protected by feelings unreplaced
On this day for you, this white rose blooms
To signify the life that remains

As this rose, so powerful yet fragile
Never takes for granted each breathe given
Receiving strength and universal understanding
Promises this rose another thousand sunrises

Hold true to your spirits
As you are in my prayers tonight
For fate has handed you this challenge
He knows above all you will conquer

And someday far in the future
When this rose finally rests
The mystery and beauty this rose possesses
Will live on eternally through the wind

Each and every single day.

Get Well.

Damn It Man

Damn it man, take a stand.
Come on boy, claim your words.
You're a coward,
This time it's over.
Out of mistakes you've made,
You'll have to wait,
I can't adhere,
I won't be coming for you.
Don't you know it's your turn?
It is up to you.
Keep on going.
Might as well tell you,
I don't care what they say
They are no one to me,
Only my enemies.
Aren't you with them?
How long will this go on?
Help me let go,
It is only fair,
Too many years,
Far too many tears.

redemption

losing all mental stability
tangible body so whole in itself
turn me down and turn me out
you were always so understanding
this hold onto this way of living
changing the past is always impossible
time to pull this game you've been playing
time to turn this thing around
now we can put forces against forces
this never was between you and I
through the wind I hear your screams
echoing in my head and slicing at my veins
i try and grasp the force in-between
So hopeless and overwhelming
my tears will no longer carry you home
i've been stripped of my emotions
you once stole my strong will
leaving me weaker than I've ever been
tomorrow is another chance for you
burn me and tie me to your wishes
these thoughts of redemption are cold
and far too far out of reach

Mislead

My hands are tied because he is hollow inside
I do not judge him, it's not my place
But I watch as all his demons come into play
I step back into my safe space, and pray he'll be okay

His shallow exterior masks his insecure heart
The evil that surrounds him has found its way in
He pushes away anyone who gets too close
He's been running so long, hiding within an empty soul

He claims he is strong, but he's just an insect following along
He lost his values along his broken path, and he doesn't care
Though I do not blame him, it's so sad I can't save him
And the truth of the matter is, so selfish within...

He won't stop long enough to save himself.

But no sorry excuse of a man will break my faith
Or break my belief in love and all good things
And karma is a bitch, boy...I've paid it many times
It hits three times harder than what you did to deserve it

White Flag

You've won
I'm gone
A white flag
I never thought
Are you happy now?
That it's impossible
Can you sleep tonight?
How does that feel?
You play the victim
As you lie and cheat
You find more ways
Continuously destroying
So, I gave you my love (shrug)
I never hid it
I told the world
No hesitation
It's so hard
Not to pick up that phone
Another holiday
Here without you

Open Door

Death does not change the way I feel
As if time really takes away the pain
So, I lie and say...I take it day by day...
But here is the thing...
There are some scars that just do not heal.
There is a type of pain that has no end
The open wound may be covered with fresh flesh
But there is a constant reminder hidden underneath
You think that I am cold, and my heart has turned to ice
Powerful yet the most powerless
Mind clear, heart uninvolved and silent
Door.... Open or locked?

Who Knows Better

So far away yet you're still right here
Running through my emotional patterns
So far from reality, putting back together my past
I've tried so hard to just forget
another lost night owned by my memory
there is nothing more there
this broken connection can't be fixed
my heart is in a wrong place
my mind has overtaken my dreams
my control had obviously failed me
your heartless hopes have broken me
I'm buried alive in this grave
blackened memories of a short-lived dream
but a dream is always inevitably ending
so, they say nothing lasts forever
it is pain and betrayal who knows better

My Love

My love for you grows each day
Even after a disagreement I find another reason to believe
I know the mind can be deceived
But our true hearts can always see
Maybe we will make it after all
The alter in the past- seemed so far
All of my dreams rest within your soul
And now I know I'm exactly where I belong

Countless times we've misplaced trust
We've traded insignificant lust for love
And now in your eyes I see forever
Though inside I've always known you're mine
I promise to give myself unselfishly
From this moment forward through eternity
Each night and every morning I'll be there
To kiss you goodnight and wish you sweet dreams
To wake you in the morning with…ssshhh… hehe
And to tell you how much I will love you always

It is You

Some answers are never found
Some words are never said
some lies are never revealed
some wounds are never healed
some hearts are never coated
some loves are never chanced
some reasons are never understood
some causes are never justified
but never say never to karma
because it will find you
and when a debt is due
and it won't be me, but you
maybe I will catch a glimpse
maybe I will have front row seats
Is it I, the fool, to believe?
Is it I, the fool, to not give in?
Is it I, the fool, to have faith?
Or is it you, the fool, to lie and deceive?
You, the fool, to stop and follow.
You, the fool, to run and cower.

FEAR

I AM AFRAID I MIGHT BE A LITTLE BIT FRIGHTENED
A CHANGE WHETHER GOOD OR BAD
IS STILL A CHANGE TO BE ADAPTED
HIDDEN AWAY AND MISSING FROM THE OBVIOUS
STILLNESS IN THE AIR BEHIND ME IN THE SHOWER
I AM WAITING FOR THE GLASS TO BREAK
HOLDING YOUR BREATH AND WATCHING FROM THE STAIRS
ANOTHER NIGHT, ANOTHER TIDAL WAVE
I AM PARANOID, BUT IT IS THE WAY I DID NOT CHOOSE TO BE
AFTERALL...
WHO KNOWS WHO IS WHO, OR WHO WON'T BUT WOULD?

SHAKEN FROM THE LIGHTNING AND THE FLOODING RAIN,
I STEPPED OUTSIDE MY WINDOW TO SEE YOU THERE
I CAN'T SPEAK BUT I CAN'T RUN AWAY
NOW I AM SUPPOSED TO LET YOU IN??
MY THOUGHTS WERE FOCUSED ON THE OPPOSITE
YOUR TOUCHES STRIKE THOUGH ME
BLOOD FROM YOUR KISS FLOWS ACROSS MY SKIN
MY FEAR LIES WITHIN YOUR CHOICES
LOOKS ARE WORDS WITH NO ACTIONS
THE SUN MIGHT TORCH MY SKIN
BUT THE HAND OF THE UNINVITED SCORNS WITHIN.

THE SWEET SURRENDER OF YOUR VENGEANCE
ALLOWED TO BE FORGOTTEN
STAKES THROUGH MY HEART, HURTING AND ALL ALONE
NOW I TAKE A STAND, SO RUN AS FAR AS YOU CAN
YOU CANNOT STOP IT FROM COMING
WHEN KARMA TAKES ITS TOLL
SHE KNOWS WHAT SHE IS COMING FOR
STEP ONE IS OVER, AND TIME MAY HAVE DISAPPEARED
SLIPPING INTO THE TURNING, YOUR THOUGHTS ARE DISSOLVED
MINE REMAIN...
FOREVER... EVERY DAY.

Notice Me

Do you notice,

When we don't talk?

Do you have urges,

You cannot stop?

Do you waste time,

Battling yourself?

Do you ever question,

How much we actually control?

February

You've taken my heart
You've taken my soul
You've taken my sanity
You've taken my power
You've taken my future
You've taken my freedom
You've taken my tears
You've taken my voice
You've taken my will
You've taken my love
You've taken my sleep
You've taken my dreams
You've taken my hope
You've taken my smile
You've taken my laugh
You've taken my thoughts
You've taken my plans
You've taken my vows
You've taken my everything
You've left with sadness
You've left me with pain
You've left me alone
You've left me broken
You've left me empty
You've left me forever
And, I still love you.

Reuniting

We loved each other's crazy
Which is very hard to find
Yes, my core is destroyed
Yes, our souls are still communicating
Your scent still sets me on fire
The sweat from your sleep on your pillow...
Sigh...
I will not be okay
But I accept this as my reality
I pray you are with me
Every second of every minute
Of every hour of every day
I will never love another
You own my heart, my body, and my thoughts
One day you will reach out to me
Our souls reuniting
And we will finally be
Together forever

Not Over Yet

Never say never they say
Never say always...
A promise intended to keep
A vow inevitably to break...
I cannot promise things I cannot give you
I cannot swear to you something I do not believe in
I want nothing more than to give you my all
But I do not have my all to give
I want nothing more than you to be as happy as you can be
But I do not know if I can hand you that happiness
My honesty might hurt you, I understand
But not as bad as a betrayed heart if I stayed
And as hard as I try to walk a straight line
Sometimes it is like someone else is controlling my thoughts
Sometimes what we believe should last forever
Does not end up the way we planned
But that does not make it any less full of love and content
If you do not give up on me... I will not give up on you
And maybe someday we will see this through
And if it does not end up how we always planned
There is a place in my heart with your name on it
For eternity... No one will ever reach it...
Not everything has to end bad
And I am not letting you go just yet
I am just preparing myself for the pain
Just in case... another round... ends the same

Pissed Off

You know what

I give up

I am damaged

It is too late

Repetition

There is no time

Cannot change

Already done

No regrets

Under my skin

Straight up

Pissed the fuck off

Not at him

Or her...

Or you...

Just myself

The Hardest

I'm waiting for the moment

I can hear your voice in the wind

And the feeling of you close to me

Shivers throughout my body

I'm not whole without you

And our souls are connected

But I'm still here…

The nightmare starts over each morning

Every single morning…

And I push through the day

But you're with me every second

I'm looking for your presence

Everywhere I go

My head pounds each night

From holding myself up each day

But still…

Watching his tears is the hardest

Story Book: Chapter One

Can I get out of the hole I've fallen in?
Can I not take the things that drive my reasons?
Can I not have these things behind my motivations?
I've survived this pain twenty times before
Though I didn't ever conquer the despair,
Because, obviously, I came back for more
This is all about me
And the person I have been molded to be
Every time something happens, and I can break free
I don't, I don't do anything, I just remain
This shelter I've grown accustomed too
This routine I've built around my heart
The fear I've engraved into my mind
And the curse that has taken me to the bottom
All these things I can see through
But I am frozen…in my own decisions
Everything I once was, has been hidden
Away from the world, and myself included

Story Book: Chapter Two

I don't know who I look at in the mirror
And my eyes even fool myself
As the days, months and years roll by
I'm standing there, fully clothed, but NAKED
I look across the room at a picture
What was once there has faded
This game we call life is just a movie
Why can't we hear them yelling...DON'T!
I've escaped into a world that is full
But it's funny that no matter what,
If you're not genuinely happy inside
A few acres worth of land, a perfect happy home
A family full of secrets, an extravagant veil
None of this can complete something missing
There is no way around this sort of emptiness
There is nothing you can steal or buy
And there's only so much denial you can stand
If you're not complete, you'll notice every day

Story Book: Chapter Three

You can love someone with all your heart
And still not be able to force yourself to be IN love
And sometime love fades away
There's no one to blame, there's no explanation
Why can't we just be happy?
Because you have got to pay your dues,
You need to accept your calling
You have something to prove... to someone
I find a sense of relief in the dark clouds outside today
Sometimes you need a little lightning and thunder
Sometimes for you to see the love you had
You must lose it first...

Story Book: Chapter Four

I put myself here
in this illusion
I do this all the time
I feel more than I learn
I thought I knew better
And yet here I am again
Wishing I'd done it differently
Or maybe wishing to do it all again
Inside I think I'm dying
But it's a good show to watch
If anyone knew me at all
They would see through my wall
But it is fine, I will be fine
I need no crutch to fall back on
I need no one to listen, no one to care
Or act like I mean so much whatsoever
Again, inside it's like I'm dying
And my blood is running thin
Again, my heart has started repeating
No one will ever get past my exterior
This is good and sad at the same time
Because I know I'll never let someone in
I won't let anyone tie me down
And have me in their sick control
But I do hope nothing else goes wrong
Not for a minute... Or I think I'll break down

They say God only gives you what you can handle
I do believe this is true... I guess I'm relied on to be strong
Or... That's just the way it is

Gold Specs

Behind his eyes

Is a broken man

Not most would notice

The gold specs fading

You are consuming me just as you always have

You cannot comprehend what you have not been through

The more darkness you try to bestow

The farther my light will extend to protect my heart

The longer you wait to open your eyes

The longer you will wait to receive my love

Impossible Vengeance

The sun rises to the occasion
When the night falls, I am here alone
I choose to be here, it is my decision
I don't want your pity, only what is owed
Any aspect of response would be sufficient

I don't want to see your face
I don't wish to hear your voice
I no longer long for your touch
And your lips don't melt me like before
I just need this to be closed

I am not breaking apart, I am just lost
I am in a bind, and you hold the ties
Pushing harder, pulling tighter
I wanted to yell, I wanted to cry
I'd like to take you behind the fire...and push you in

Burn you as you have burned me
Blacken your skin to match my heart
And to think I do not give a fuck
This is my impossible vengeance

Silent Noise

My heart was unprotected from your grip, and scarred from your manipulations

The silence was louder than all the noise, and cut far deeper than your words

You claimed to be strong, but you were weaker than the rest

I claimed to be weak, but my strength was just hiding within my fear

You didn't take me down; it was just a mountain in the road I had to climb

I've overcome far worse than you, it was just a test for myself to see the truth

With no regrets you took from me what did not belong to you in the first place

You took advantage of every facet of my being and worse, you enjoyed it

Every day you found a way to take me down and make me notice

Your affection was non-existent, and our love suffered from it

You questioned my every move while you reveled in your double-standards

You whispered to me in my sleep, you'd kill me if I ever tried to leave

I tried to play pretend and not understand as if you were speaking another language

You thought I didn't know the thoughts you were thinking but your eyes told the story

I misjudged the seriousness of the situation as if it were involuntary

I escaped a horrific fate, but I will never forget the teachings of survival

It's A Thin Line

I love the way you take me down
I love the way you take control
I love the way you don't give up
I love the way you try to pretend you're not in

I hate the way you look at me
I hate the way you try to deceive
I hate the way you lie so easily
I hate the way I love the things I hate

I love the way you hold me down
I love the way you let me take control
I love the way you don't give in
I love the way you try to pretend you're out

I hate the way you can take me down
I hate the way you make me feel
I hate the way your kiss melts me
I hate the way I love the things I want

I love the way I run the other way
I love the way I fool myself
I love the way I just give in
I love the way I pretend I'm not

I hate the way I run away
I hate the way I deny you the right
I hate the way I'm such a bitch
I hate the way I hate the things I love

I love the way you try to hide
I love the way you try to run
I love the way you screw me over
I love the way it's all a game

I hate the way I'm in your thoughts
I hate the way I'm in your dreams
I hate the way I'm in your heart
You hate the way you're in love

Silly Boy

Prying to get inside my thoughts
I am stuck here on your web
You were so nervous lying next to me
Could it be...
You have started to break
You have no clue of who I am
Who are you...
But a selfish liar covered by a rock star persona
Do you think they actually care?
You're wrong right along with me
As long as we can keep this going
It still could never be
You and me
Inside a dream
So, so far...
From reality
If we can run away
As far as we can get
Even with nowhere to turn
Alone we could learn
Who are we trying to fool?
You are not in my heart
My hate could always be true
You've actually started to feel
Have I shadowed your emotional walls of detachment?

This Battle

This battle is between the forces of good and evil

It was never between you and I

I will never admit how good it felt

You will never see that look in my eyes

You will never feel my heart racing as it is

Your hand will never melt me to the ground as well

The rain cleanses my skin of your touch

Someone else's sweat cleansing my thoughts

You don't want to know that someone else

Is inside of me doing the things you did

How tight my legs wrap around their hips

Or their fingers running over my lips

That kiss you will never feel again

All the pleasure I once proclaimed

The warmth surrounding your... ssshhh

...You need not fear anymore scars

Each scar that was a tear in my heart

I can't seem to sleep anymore

Because my mind won't stop running

Analyzing each one of my thoughts

To the point of regression

Hmmm.... It could get aggressive

Take me on if you wish, I will never give in

The Difference

We are all deceived by the thought
That life is what you make it
Sometimes life can be cruel
Others might not think like you
Then you're stuck alone again
Wallowing in your own self-sacrifices
Everywhere is the same
The people and the places
Everyone thinks for themselves
No one has a conscience
You could follow your dreams
But where do they lead
Into another foolish hope
To later be shattered
We all want too much
We don't keep what's worth it
We seem to push away
Things that could make a difference
Then we are all alone again
Crushed and shattered
Lying in our heads
Alone with only a wish
I wish that something could be
Maybe more than a dream
I'm starting to realize the similarity
Neither one exists
A dream and a wish
Things to make us think
Life can be what we make it
There are always going to sorrows
Why would I see these dreams in my head?
Why do I feel this fear in my veins?
I want too much, I expect too little

you're a fool

oh, i like it

give me more

i can take it

look inside

who brought you out

you fell into

another web

you forgot the rules

how could you?

you will learn

An Innocent Heart

Then there was dark

There was nothing more

No explanations why

No love left to be found

Someone broke an innocent heart

It is I who understands

Innocent once my heart was

Then someone I thought I could trust came along

In the magic of the moment, I forgot

I let go of everything I had ever been taught

Now it appears too late for mine

So, take your broken heart and fly

Don't think again of this terrorized pain

It seems impossible for me to learn

Don't follow where you know there's hurt

I've been told it's all for nothing

But what I've found more true than most

The more pure your heart is found to be

The more easily the vultures come to feed

And as often as a baby cries

Another innocent heart must die

Crucified and trampled trying to understand

We have no say in this bullshit anyway

We cannot blame and we cannot forsake

We can only try not to make the same mistake

Try to see the ones you think are your enemies

Are just the ones that have felt your pain

Trying to protect you from feeling it again

Maybe what they've felt is far worse in the first place

So maybe we can make our own mistakes

Even when it's our own innocent heart that must break again

Was it You?

Should I feel sorry for you?
Are you drowning in your mistakes?
Are the nightmares taking over your sleep?
Have you begun to feel the pain?
As I crumbled and as you watched me burn,
Was it easy for you to do?

You left me alone to figure it out... Why?
I just wanted the truth... Was it you?

Sleepless Minutes

By myself and hurting
Not able to sleep
Tossing and turning
Making wishes of impossibilities
I hear your voice
It comforts me
The thought of being away
Bringing these tears I'm crying
Somewhere out there
Where you are sleeping
I can't keep warm
Watching the minutes pass
Wondering what you're doing
If you're thinking of me
Even though I am so tired
No way can I sleep

Nothing To Say

The rain washes away your face

Imperfections of what you were supposed to be

Standing naked I wait for an answer

I want to know why

You hurt me in this way

I want to know why

You left me to deteriorate

I want to know why

You have nothing to say

Touched By an Angel

Though your time has come

To travel on without us

You have left behind a legacy

Never ever even knowing

How many lives you have touched

How many lifted by your kindness

You brightened each of our lives

In far too many ways to count

Your graciousness remains

And though we all know you are in a better place

Each day we will think of you

And tears may be shed

Knowing you are looking down

Still ready to lend a hand

It is enough to know one day we will meet again

And until then we extend our love

And thank you for being who you were

We were blessed by God to have known you

Each of us knowing we were touched by an angel

This Pain

I watched you walk away
You risked everything
My strength held my tears
My belief held my strength
I will wait for the day
You come to me
We will kiss forever
I will finally understand
All the pain that kept me waiting

The pages inside of our covers
Differ in many ways
But pain is pain
And tears come in many forms
I will remember
It is not forever

I feel our fate, our destiny
It seems unbelievable
Time plays with our hearts
All my dreams pass me by
Have I given up?
Or is it I have given in?

Live is a struggle
Everyone understands this
In the end, as long as we are together
I will live each day as if it was tomorrow
You come to me
And now we can see
Nothing comes easily
Unconditional love cannot be broken
It is ours, finally

The tears build behind my eyes
I deny them their right
Are you thinking of me tonight?
I have given all of me
Everything inside available to give
Despite all of the shit
I will never give up on this
God works in mysterious ways
I know he will bring you back to me
This is where you belong
Here, tightly wrapped in my arms

Stay Calm

I'm angry
I admit it
I'm trying to stay calm
It's so damn hard
I made a vow
To protect him
Why is it now
I'm protecting him from you?
Do you see?
The problem created
You're part of his world
You're giving up his love
It might not matter to you
It might seem petty
To him it means the world
Maybe if you would think
Stop being so selfish
You'd realize the angel
Calling out your name
The angel of honor
You don't even deserve him

I Question You This

If you're not happy, then why do you stay?

If there's something you're wanting, why not go after it?

If courage is stronger than fear,

If love is stronger than hate,

If a feeling is stronger than your restraint...

How much sense does it all make?

Everyone thinks it's all about them,

And if you're sad, what is it that makes you happy?

If you need a release, where do you get it?

If it's really all out of our control, why does it happen?

How do you fill an empty space, if you're not quite sure what it would take?

When you need a break from it all, where do you run?

Walk Away

If I am feeling good, why does it always rain?
But when I am sad, the sun does not shine
If we made our own choices,
Why choose to be in this predicament?
Who I was yesterday is not who I am today
And tomorrow I will be somebody else completely
I do not hide behind make-up
But I hide behind my heart
If it could be opened again, would I accept that?
No…I would not.
I will never let you in
I will never trust anyone again
I have no love to share
I have no happiness to give
I have nothing you can take from me
Just walk away.

Nothing You Can Buy Me

No amount of diamonds
Or acres of land
No matter how many bedrooms
Or cars in the drive
A walk-in closet... Three full baths... 52-inch LCD TV's...
It does not matter
When I am lying on my deathbed
And I take a look back
I do not want to remember these material objects
As how I lived my life
I am not settling for money
Or a multi-story mansion
There is nothing you can buy me
To replace the love I crave
There is no amount of money
You could give me... More than what I need
Nights on the front porch
Watching the clouds wander by
The arms of someone who loves me
Holding me tight
Someone to be there
If tears shall shed
Someone to pick me up
If I happen to fall
Someone who loves me enough
To walk the beach at sunset
With nothing else but... Me...
Do you not see?
There is nothing you could buy me
That I do not have already
Or could not attain by myself
Except some kind of bandage
To mend my broken heart
I haven't let go of my beliefs
But I am finding... They are fading...
With each person that I meet
And maybe there is no one else out there
Like me...

Scattered

Shivering, aching, slipping away, I can't stay
Tossing, turning, falling back, I can't sleep
Harming, fading, wanting more, I can't leave
Crying, trying, dying more, I can't forget
I can't again, giving nothing, expecting at all

I have nothing to give
You've taken it all
I gave you everything
You still want more

Bleeding, turning, dreaming truth, I can't wait
Sweating, fainting, burning more, I can't forget
Analyzing, regretting, lacking hope, I can't remember
Watching, taunting, making excuses, I can't hear
I can't to give, giving nothing, expecting it all

I have nothing to give
You've taken it all
I gave you everything
You still want more

Taking, faking, pretending, calling, begging, stealing, lying,
freezing, Crawling, breaking,
Forsaking

Stolen Again

My beauty does nothing kill me
Taunting my innocence
I wait to be healed, somehow
Someone to look deeper
Lead me to where I'm meant to be
I wait patiently
For I know nothing in life is free
For I know nothing comes easily

You prayed for beauty in haste
But it's the look that brings deceit
And when it is said and done
It's all just to get inside
The beauty within you
Is completely passed by
For I know where I've been
For I know the pain in the end

Trust

I have to admit

I'm getting nervous

The look in your eyes

I've never seen before

The evil in your strength

Is working with your mind

What are you planning?

How far would you go?

To stop me from leaving

You did this to yourself

You're terrifying me with

The touch of your hand

I see you breaking

How could you do this?

I've got to get away

I might never get the chance

Help me someone

Hear my silent screams

The one I once trusted

Is going to stop me

From ever being able

To breathe again

J

Why must it be this way?
Why must it be you or I?
One of us always giving
One of us always taking
Never at the same time uniting
It must be a rare kind of sickness
A special kind of toxic love
Will it ever be the right timing?
When we both give and take as one
They say it's consistent with insanity
For you and I to even try again
Is there an ultimate lesson?
Or is it always this ultimatum between now and never?

It would be so easy for me to be,
Consumed by your narcissism once again
So easy for me to flip that switch,
To not take no for an answer and rush in
To again lose myself in your selfishness
To cry, to hurt, to feel the numbness taking over,
To give in to the emptiness you're taunting me with
I'm not sure if it's self-sabotage or my intuition trying to protect me
I don't understand your actions, but do I even understand my own?

I do know I'm not in the mood

I Gave In

History repeats and there I go again
Is change my guilty pleasure or my enemy
Why when it is out of my reach…
Do I take it as a challenge I have got to conquer
But when it is in my hands, I push it away as if it means nothing
Even if in the process I ruin everything

This is how my mind used to work
Before I started to listen to God's lessons
Could people see through my fake smile?
Could they hear the meaning in-between my words?
And if it appears I am falling, I am not, I'm lying
As the sun scorched my skin, I gave in

it is in a name

Keeping our love close to my heart
Endings like this are always hard
Vulnerable to your touch, yes
It just wasn't the right time for us
Now I know it was unconditional

Couldn't you see me fading?
Are you that blind?
Reality is always a shock if you are not
Listening...

All the years I sacrificed
Letting go of all of my fears
Everything was for nothing
eXhausted and exhilarating at the same time
And I thought I knew you
Now I'm playing the fool
Darkness hid the truth I was hiding
Every day there was something new
Revealed within my words is my heart

Remember everything we made
Hold each single memory deep within
It will never be goodbye between you and I
Never let go of what we shared
Every day it will remain in me

I thank you.

WHAT I GET

No more
Make it stop
End this
Leave me alone
You see
What it's doing
To me
I can't take it
Stay aware
I've been blinded
Fight harder
I've been trying
Many lessons
Not needed
Telling me
I deserve it
Any closer
I'd be dying.

No Worries

I get it
I'm gone
No worries
Promise this
It sucks
I know
Nothing left
To pull us back
One loss for a gain
There is a problem
I can't adhere
You're make believe
I made you real
I am done
I cannot take it
I will leave
You'll regret it
It is hard to say
What made this
We both know
The obstacles
It was impossible
Seems too far away
In my reality
We could have done it

But what can I say?

I wouldn't have given it all up anyway

This Night

I am trying to forget everything you promised

Learning to get through the day alone

I lay awake in my bed night after night in distress

For this I may have regret

The tears I cry turn to dust

I have given up

As the days continue to build up

It's hard to tell if it's getting any easier

Some days I feel as if I could conquer the world

Some days I feel as if I could disappear

I am trying to forget everything you ever said

Pretending this never even happened

There is a part of my life I'd now take back

For this I can't forgive you

The tears I cry turn to dust

I have given up

Skin Deep

You say I need to relax

I am feeling just fine

You follow me home

You say so I am not alone

You tell me not to worry

While your ulterior motives are brewing

Yet all my control has been stolen

I feel sick

Problem rising

Who the hell can we trust

If we cannot trust the ones we love

And how many times will we be deceived

Before we realize emotions are only skin deep

The Battle Between Myself and I

I feel this...   this isn't real
I need that...   that is untouchable
I am in pain... pain is an illusion
I trust...   I do not
I dream...   covered in blood
I cry tears...   tears of darkness
I tell myself... none of it matters
It comes... it goes... it never stays long
Long enough to feel... but feel what?
Love is also an illusion...   the fear of losing
When you cannot have it...   you just want it more
When it is on the table...   you want far from it
Over and over I fight... I'm constantly changing my mind
I am happy... I am sad
I'm angry...   I'm just fine
It is alive...   resting inside
Waiting for you...   I'm in hiding
Another day... gone forever
The past...   never changes

A Special Thank you

Each time we pray
What we think is a meaningless prayer
Each time we didn't receive
What we begged and pleaded for
We live in haste
We take so much for granted
We do not always remember
Everything he has done for us
Every unanswered prayer
Was just to help and guide us
Not to make us feel misery
I want to thank him
For all the times
I thought he wasn't there
I thought he didn't care
It turns out he always was
Watching over me
Knowing what choices I made
Knowing that the things that I needed
Were not the things I thought I wanted
And now I look back on all the years
Another way to help us
I was blinded by selfishness
For all those prayers
He could not answer

I Am Bound

I block you out
I bind you down.
I hold your thoughts
You disappoint.
I stick around
I play the part.
You disappear
I believe your lies.
When I run
You pull me back.
When I stay
You push me away.
I hold my ground
I put down my pride.
I do not ask why
You do it again.
You make me the fool
When it is really all you.
It is me who can see inside
It is you who can con them all.
Because my conviction
Is stronger than your will.
Because my beliefs
Are stronger than your guiles.
Because I choose to face my karma
And you choose to run and hide.
Because I choose to believe in your good
You chose to break me open.
and break me apart.
You pushed and you pushed
To string me along
You are regret.
You just do not see
The time will come
it becomes so clear.

Shed No Tears

If my time here is through

I will live on forever within you

I'm always just a breath away

Close your eyes and there I stand

Shed no tears and wear no frown

I made the best of it while I could

I will live on forever within you

Predicament

I am trying to paint on a smile

But my eyes tell the story of our love

Each morning the pain starts over

Each night I'm crying out for you

I'm just going through the motions

I've learned so well day to day

Inside my heart is not beating

My core is ripped to shreds

The silence is deafening

But I can't bear to hear a sound

There is literally no way to describe

This feeling inside of me

No words to define

There's just no way I could

And I've already fucking told you

You're the only one who could take it away

So, it's quite the predicament

You have put me in once again

Except there's not a fucking thing I can do

To piece us back together once more

Karma: Past

We have all done things
We didn't mean to do
Some of these things hurt others
Some of these things hurt only you
When you knew what you were doing
Without a sense of reason
This is when a mistake turns into betrayal
And betrayal turned into guilt
Guilt turned into pain within ourselves
And to determine if those reasons
Were just circumstantial to someone else
Basically, was that your decision to make?
And this is when karma came into play
Karma, fate, and destiny have always had a pact
The universe was always watching
And whether that is good or bad
Right or wrong or somewhere in-between
Meant to happen or just a game
It is true what they say my friend
What goes around comes around
You have learned.

Karma: Present

What goes around comes around…
Or so they say
Even the purest of hearts
Can be misled
To do just something right
And think that's that
This isn't the way
That karma plays
One thing I know
And I know it for certain
And the reason I know
Is I've paid it before
So, if you fuck me over
And leave me to drain
Fuck with my heart
And leave me to bleed
Although I may be angry
I won't ever wish misfortune
On anyone at any time
I now play by karmas rules
If it is so, and you have a due to pay
It won't be me, and I won't be there
So, none of this matters anyhow
Because I know you will know why
When the moment hits
Karma decides it's your turn
The time has come, your hand is dealt

Roses Burst Into Flames

I'm watchin' the sun come up and I feel at peace
It's all gonna work itself out because it's in God's hands
I see what you were tryin' to do, getting' me all worked up
But it's not workin' this time, my heads not slippin' into your lies

What used to drive me crazy and send me spiraling into chaos
I just shake my head, you can do your own thing,
because I'm not playin' into your gamin' ways
I can hear the crickets chirping, girl you don't need that kind of stressin'
And it feels damn good to not even care a little

What you expected me to do is come back cryin',
I guess this time the jokes on you, because I'm still smilin'
You handed me roses, minutes later they burst into flames
Goodbye is just a chance for new hellos, so I'm saying my final goodbye to you

October

A year ago, I could have never dreamt
To be where I am now
Where I wake up
Isn't always where I lay down
To these questions
I have no answers
Tomorrow the sun will rise again
I'll be here, still running around

In the darkness, in my head

To you I owe nothing
For you I'll take nothing
I have no last requests
I have no worries, no regrets
I know as well as you
That we are not meant
Even though it's not what I wanted
It's just the way it is, and it is shit

Just last night I wondered
What you might be up to
I thought about picking up that phone
Couldn't make myself do it
To these fears
I have no reasons
The moon will fall again tonight
The light shining on our memories

In the darkness, in my head

I Will See You There

Falling out of love into misery
Why do I need an explanation?
I cannot wait now
For another drained out reaction
What test is this?
Who is coming next?
What lesson am I learning?
I'm tormented all the time
This is my converted armor...ching-ching
I've lost another
This game must end forever
Can't you see I'm losing it now?
I need your focus....

Tempting and feeding my directions
Crawling and starving for information
Smoking away my sense of compassion
Alluring and killing chances of being whole
Swallowing and choking on your pleasure
It's not all good for you can never be sure
Fuck your emotional traumas
Such a waste of worn conversation
I'll never accept all of these excuses...

If I go to Hell, I will see you there.

THIS IS ME

Step away I warn you
I'm about to break
When it seems, I've had too much
I try to breathe it all in
Sometimes it helps
Other times I fall
Either way it doesn't matter
Everything is coming down

I feel you coming out
Was there something you wanted to say
Fearful motives covered by hope
Empty touches, empty promises
I've hurt my muscles
Stretching too thin
Oh, fucking well
It doesn't matter anyhow

Too many problems, not enough answers

GONE

Give it up
Let me be
I will hurt you
I am not afraid
I have been wrong
I have been cheated
No more dreams
No more chances
This is gonna stop
I am going to break
You are so beautiful
In the moon's light
None of this matters
You're alone tonight
Don't call on me
I won't be home
Don't leave me alone
I am waiting for nothing
It is coming down
Way too fast
I can't keep up
I am losing control
I lost the motivation
A long time ago
You stole my emotions
You had no clue
Now I do
So let me go
Someday ahead of time
Maybe then I will forgive
But even if I did
I still won't forget the pain

Think Before You Act

Everyone has an opinion
You can always be swayed
Out of your own decisions
What you know is real
Before you realize
You have changed her mind
We're all left alone
Habits we can't break
Nothing lasts forever
I stand alone

Everything stop
I'm going insane
A thousand different thoughts
Remain unchanging
Handle it all
He calls out to me
Like I'm enjoying
Going insane

Forget what I said
Forget what I promised
Forget what I thought I meant
It's not only you that's hurting
It may have been my choice
But you pushed me to it

Smiling

You heed no warnings I sent out
You don't believe I know myself?
You don't know me at all
I don't know you anymore

I don't want anyone standing above me
I don't really want anyone beside me
I stand alone, I'm content
What's the use of being unhappy?

Yesterday I smiled all day
And the day before I felt the same way
I am happy within myself
Life's too short to not do what you want

They Fucking Lied

When they told me
It's never too late
They lied
When they told me
Your heart will go on
They lied
When they told me
I'd be okay one day
They lied
When they told me
It would get better
They lied
When they told me
I would love again
They lied
They fucking lied

The Exact Thing

The only things I couldn't take
Is that exact thing you've done to me
Tell me, how am I supposed to respond?
What reaction were you expecting exactly?
Did you think that by you being a coward,
That I wouldn't still feel the burn?
You are hiding from everyone you know
Tell me, is there anyone in the world,
Who knows who you really are?
Or are you just that damn good?
Could it be that I am the only one,
Who can see through your exterior?
I know inside you have a heart that beats
But I suppose you have masked it very well
Shallow and selfish actions
Followed by regret and remorse
I have the purest of pure hearts
And you, my friend, have broken it
So, whatever your reasons are
And whatever you tell everyone else
I hope it is worth it in the end
Because I know, I am who I am
And I know exactly what I am worth
And I realize I am a little crazy
And I know at times I jump the gun
I have flaws and faults and am far too outspoken
I get far too emotional at times when I am drunk
And yes, id kick another girl's ass for intruding
But I am loyal and honest and ambitious
And I am warm and sweet and dedicated
And don't I know I can be a complete bitch
But I feel horrible about it within minutes
I'm an awesome friend and my kids are my life
Forget it, it's my turn to apologize
I am sorry I gave you someone worth loving
And I am sorry I let you see into my heart
Above all, I am sorry because it is the rarest of defeat
I let myself fall in love.... With you.

Hurt Me If You Will

My body aches...
My mind needs a break.
I'm past the point of delirium...
And it feels kinda nice.

Nothing matters at this point...
You could stab me again.
I probably wouldn't even notice...
So... take your aim... let it slide in.

I'm sure people on the outside looking in...
Wonder what it was that messed me up.
Don't let him take you down again (they keep saying)
As if I had a choice in the matter.

If I was who I used to be...
I would take you down myself.
Start at the bottom... make my way back up...
I used to not wait for karma... But now I've learned.

Karma is more of a bitch than I...
And will make more things occur.
And it is her that decides when and how...
You will pay your dues... And I love it.

So... Hurt me again if you will...
Talk your shit... keep lying to yourself.
Pretend it's all me... It's all me...
Is this as hard as it gets?? I will tell you what.

Do Not Stop

You overtook my power
I had no control
But I did not even want it
I am yours
I felt your breath on my neck
I felt the weight of your soul
It is a feeling deep inside
I cannot quite explain it
But I know you feel it too
Our hearts connecting
Through the air
On another level
I give in to my deepest desires
And id give anything for it to be real
You can feel me
And I can feel you
And I whisper how much I need you
And have I told you lately how much I love you
Now you know… now you see…
You see all of me
I see all of you
Do not stop.

Words

You say the things you don't mean; you mean the things you don't say
I lost it all when I let you in, I forgot to tell you what I meant
When I say that's it's not you, I lie, you're the only reason why

You pretend things aren't as they are, you think it's yours when it's not
The last time ended when we said goodbye, I know it's hard to live a lie
When I say that it's not you, I lie, you're the only reason why

You pretend to be someone you're not; you fight everyday being someone else
If you saw the person I see inside, the person you keep well hidden behind you lies
You're consumed by things that don't exist; you create a life that isn't real

Take A Bow

What you thought you knew of me
Was the illusion I led you to believe
In my head, the thoughts spin
Too fast for you to catch a glimpse
Here I am again... Nothing but a shell
Surrounding a battered heart
Bruised ego, and altered trust
Over and over, I put the fires out
Again and again, I take a bow
These people that come and go
Destined to be just a memory
Programmed to do what they are told
So sadly, taken over by false words
Steadily I watch them run
Back and forth between others
Is it I, who wants too much?
Or is it them, who do not want enough?

With Me

I burned myself today

I said everything I didn't mean

Why do I run away?

Why is it nice words scare the Hell out of me?

My heart was blackened a long time ago

My trust has failed me too many times

If I tell you I like being closed up, I am lying

If I tell you I feel no emotions, I'm being honest

If no one can get through

No one can cause you pain

Even if it is unintentional

Shit happens and I don't want it

This state of mind, I kinda enjoy it

As if nothing matters, no care in the world

It's another mask I wear to protect myself

From vultures like you

I do it all

I make things the way they are

And I don't even notice I do it

It's just how it ends...

With me.

A Reason

Was there a reason you stayed so long?

Pretending to be someone you are not?

Stealing my smile and throwing me down

You walked away, you just walked out

You left me with nothing

Except these unwanted memories

Some things are easier said than done

And some things are easier done than said

But it doesn't make it right to not let me in

I need to know what's behind this fight

If it was me, or just you not handling what you made

Like every other time I pleaded and cried

I can't believe I fell for this again

All your lies, everything you kept inside

I know it's time for me to go

It's just so damn hard to close that door

You Made Me Do This

Will you hate me tomorrow?
For what I do today
Will you try and blame me?
For the games you played
Will you run like a little bitch?
For what you put me through
Will you face duplicity?
For this heart you shattered
I always believed in you
And you broke me into pieces

I know this for sure
The only thing that's killing you is me
And the same is true
The only thing that's killing me is you

Trust Your Heart

Even though sometimes it's hard to follow
When you don't know what it's trying to say
Clear your mind and look in from the outside
Because your heart knows no boundaries
You don't have to worry about making the wrong decision
Clear your mind and let your instincts guide you

If you are gonna make it somewhere
Make it for yourself
No one is guaranteed to be there when it all comes down
No one has to care

WELL?!?

If you could imagine
For a moment
How would you feel if it were me?
Feel my pain?
Will I feel yours?
Have I felt yours?
I would go through it
just for even the chance
We will be together again
I don't want you to ever feel an ounce of pain
And I do pray for your peace
But I can't just let you go like that
And part of me needs you to see
The wreck I am
Wipe away my tears
Lay your head on my shoulder
I will wipe yours away the same
I will forever love you

NO

Maybe it's not what you expected
Maybe you expect too much
This is something I can't get over
The constant pressure on my heart
If the rain would clear, I could see the sun
But the memories the light holds
Reminds me of the darkness you embrace
When our emotions have been drained
And there is nowhere left to turn
Someone remembers what you tried to forget
Compelled to feel

Permission

I cannot expect you to stay with me forever
I would never ask that of you
But I sure as hell need you now more than ever
And if it's okay, will you stay with me for a while?
You could not wait for me in this life
But please, please wait for me before our next
And I am so sorry I let you down
Please, please, please forgive me...
But I do not get another chance
Like I have always given to you
And as if it was in my control
I was scared and thought we had forever
I took you always being there for granted
But you stole my future from me.

And I did not give you permission

Fresh Pain

Can you hear me?
How many times I call out for you?
The *I love you* I whisper before I fall asleep.
Can you see me?
The tears that rain down my cheeks.
Can you feel me?
The emptiness within me--This is you.

Why didn't I hear you?
As you called out for me.
The *I love you* you whispered before you fell asleep.
Why couldn't I see you?
The tears that rained down your cheeks.
Why couldn't I feel you?
The emptiness within you--That was me.

You found a way to block me,
Which had to be an extremely hard thing to do.
You must have found a loophole in our soul contract,
Being there is no stronger connection than between me and you.

Your heart was bleeding out for me...
My heart is bleeding out for you...

Opposites

I should have known better, I should have seen, I can be so hard on myself, I am used to this strain, I am in need, I cannot stop, if this were you, what would you do? Stand tall, rule your world, all this shit has got to go, Who I am isn't who I used to be, I just can't understand, it's not what I wanted, you made this, Deal with it

Wonders...
Running around
Inside my head
Pulling me down
Watching me fall
Waiting at the bottom
The days are fading
Dreams are dying

You should have known better, you should have seen, you thought I would stay, you should have thought again, I am in need, if this were me, what would you do? You'd run away, you'd hide again, where is all your strength now, the strength you put onto me, Funny how, starting now, it has all gone, it's all done, You're all alone

Haylee

Dry your eyes
The sun will shine
The years misplaced
The memories saved
A rainbow awaits you
Just around the dawn
The darkness that surrounds you
It is just for the moment
It will get better
Though I know you can't feel it
You are strong and you will survive
Through this and everything ahead
My hearts bleeds for you
And believe me if I could
I'd take away your sadness
I'd hide it all away
I'd walk your path for you
Until the end of this
To each morning you wake hurting
And each night you fight forgetting
For each tear your eyes shed
For each smile being stolen
Just know:
I'm here, and will always be
Until deaths angel kisses me
I'll be right by your side
Through all your despair
And as you know, just like they say
Every silver lining has a touch of gray

Versus

I am so tired,
> but cannot sleep

I am so hungry,
> but cannot eat

I am so angry,
> but cannot vent

I am so hurt,
> but cannot mend

I am so confused,
> but cannot tell

I am so wrong,
> but cannot change

I am the prey
> and you are the vulture

I am the Jester
> and you are the King

I am not your possession
> and you are not my passion

I am not the one you should betray
> and you cannot escape your fate

I am someone you will never comprehend
> and you are someone I will never understand

I am someone you will never keep
> and you are someone I will never take

I am someone who will love forever
> and you are someone who will never be welcome

Contradictory

I can be wicked
I know how to lie
I can be deceitful
I know how to cry
I can be crazy
I know how to yell
I can be jealous
I know how to fight
I can be revengeful
But it is not who I am
I can keep secrets
I know how to hide
I can be your worst nightmare
I can be your greatest dream
I can push your buttons
I have learned them very well
I can keep quiet
And You will never know what I am thinking
I can pretend
I can push you away
I know when to let you be
I know when to have your back
I can burn like fire
I can be as cold as ice
I can do anything
I cannot do anything
I can make myself hate you
I can wear a perfect smile
I can make myself love you
Because I cannot really make myself not
I can change my mind
At any given point of time
I can be extremely patient
I can have no patience at all
I can be ridiculously bitchy
I can be pathetically loving
I can be a damsel in distress
Or a dominating woman
I can be innocent and sweet
I can be the most aggressive girl you have met
I can be weak and melt in your arms
I can be so stubborn, and you would never know
I can be outspoken and loud
I can be so afraid and never speak a word
I can be a lady...and I can be a ....
In other words. This is it...this is who I am
You cannot change me... but I am not that bad

Hard to Follow

I felt too fast
  you fell out
    turn to leave
      you're running back
        when I need you
          you're far away
            when I'm leaving
              you beg me to stay
                I am a little confused
                  could you please explain?
                    I must be missing something
                      because this just doesn't make any sense

I love
  you hate
    I'm angry
      you're in tears
        I run
          you beg
            I stay
              you walk away
                is this it all?
                  if it is
                    lead me away
                      I can't take it again

am I the only one?
  I don't understand
    giving all I can
      it's not enough
      give nothing
      walk away
        everything's turning
        they're in love
          you're in lust
            could you please explain?
              I must be missing something
                because this just doesn't make any sense

Sweet **Darkness**

There will always be sweet darkness
There will always be unspoken words
There will always be love we never gave
There will always be the love we made
You have changed
I have changed
But, we have not
The emptiness inside my stomach
The pain in my head
My heart and mind fighting as usual
But it always ends the same
There is only one thing stronger than my love
The loathing of the feeling I have right now

Lesson Learned

So much to say, so little time left
What you long to hear, isn't always what is said
You think you are alone, there is no turning back
Remember so many of us suffer
No one to make us forget
The reason behind your bruising
Why your heart is breaking
Have you ever watched yourself cry?
Have you ever looked inside your tears?
To see what you're looking for
Maybe even exactly what it is you fear
How do you know what is within you?
You keep well hidden from the world
It will never let you go
In the end you won't be happy
Staying sad and confused
In dreams of how you want it to be
Instead of paying attention
To your own need of reality
What they say is true about hurt
Isn't necessarily what you're feeling
What they say is true about love
Isn't necessarily what your love is
If you're under someone else's hand
You will never find the meaning for yourself
We are all different in our own ways
Just as the love we give and take
Because we're all guilty of being afraid
To lose those feelings in the first place
What you're feeling might not be
Worth the pain you're feeding into
No one can judge you when they haven't walked in your shoes
They are being protected from the damage inflicted
And when the only one who can take away your pain
Is the one who made you feel that way
I don't know what to tell you
Don't be blinded
By the love you've been stealing

Nothing But a Dream

I might be making a mistake
Maybe the biggest one yet
Is this me coming through?
Who is it thinking this way?
I'm lost within my own desires
I don't know, anymore, what I want
But, I do know one thing for sure
You are so many of the reasons I'm where I'm at

I think of your inner demons
They are taking over your outer appearance
Who am I to break up a union,
Of untrusting motives and unbearable words
Of hopeless equations and questionable views
Dreaming nothing but a dream

Prisoner

An angry smile
A calm anxiety
A disdain for love
A saddened hope
A blip of understanding
Momentarily open
Pulling back in
Exhausted and wide awake
Staying patient while eager
A book from the past seeing the future
Not having a say in your own life
All the power over yourself
Remembering while trying to forget
The best for you is the worst for you
As you hide in a wide-open field
The Desire and revulsion
The restraint for freedom
The silence brings echoes
The darkness can be beautiful
Shadows with no light

Recurring Moments

I cannot just sit here,
But I cannot move.
I wait and watch for signs you are here,
And I pray I do not miss them.
Am I really feeling you near me?
Or am I creating it all in my psychosis?
Do you still want to be with me forever?
And if you do, would God allow it?
Can you still feel the depth of my love?
Are you allowed to feel desire?
It has always been me and you,
So, what in the fuck am I supposed to do?
I have never felt despair and agony like this...
And you are the only one that can heal that in me.
We can now feel one another's pain,
But you are not there for me to run to anymore,
And that is something I cannot handle.
So, I will stay here in this sorrow,
And wait for the day my tears run dry,
Though still falling.
My heart will forever remain hollow,
There is no way to fill the hole you have left in it.
You will always be the love of my life,
And do not worry baby,
There is no distance that could keep our souls apart,
Even that between Heaven and Earth.

Scarred For Life

She worries until she is sick
She cannot question her motives
It could happen again
She wonders if the pain will go away
Being there is hurting more than leaving
She tells everyone it is not as hard as it seems
As she cries herself to sleep
She is drowning in her own tears
The lies she cannot kill
Buried in his control
She knows what to do
But her fear is too strong

When the day starts
Inside a battered memory
Nearly lifeless and terrified
She tries to beat his game
No matter how good she tries to be
She just does not see
It is not her words or actions
That can stop time from repeating
Physical scars may go away
But emotionally you are scarred for life

Trying Too Hard

My heart turned cold
Filled with remorse
Aching for some kind of healing
Hopeful yet surrounded by harm
Breaking into many pieces
Impossible dreams turned to stone
Striving to survive through this
Another day to get through
When I awake and you weren't there
It was the beginning of the end

Hold me tight tonight
Tomorrow it will be gone
There is no more will to fight
There are no more chances to ruin
Failing to give us what we want
Waiting to see what is in store
For these hearts of stone
Cannot find their way back to one another

Drowning in the quicksand
Finding no resolution to this problem
I will continue to fight for myself
You have taught me one important thing
No matter how hard you try
It doesn't mean shit in the end
There is no line between love and hate
We will all still fade away
Dreams don't ruin our fate
That would be believing in it in the first place

Wake-Up

Neither here nor there

In-between love and hate

Hiding within the emotional and physical

Pushing someone away

Doesn't erase their memory

Doesn't erase their touch

Doesn't make them disappear

Doesn't make you forget

I can't stand the silence

As I sit here in the dark

A single candle burning

Your face within the smoke

I can't stand the darkness

As I sit here in the silence

A single thought repeating

You've come back for more

At times I want to sleep it off

Wake up as if it never happened

Sometimes I only want to run

Run right into your arms

I Evoke You

I drove by your old place
I went to your Quiktrip
I hung out at your skate park
I invoked our memories
I went to your house
I vacuumed up your cigarette ashes
I walked your halls
I took a deep breath
I walked down those stairs
I surveyed every foot of concreate
I took everything in, every angle
I stood where you last stood
I saw what you last saw
I felt you go through me
I felt your tears falling
I walked out on the deck
I took a memory photo
Of the view outside your kitchen window
I traced your steps
I breathed your air
I took in every single moment
You have been consumed in
I watched the lights reflect upon the water
Let the stars in the sky sink into my memory
Because I knew they had been engraved in yours
I drove the route you took to work
I memorized all of the billboards
I did everything I could possibly think of
To be there for you to attach to
And it is selfish of me, I know
But I do not care, even a little

WISH

The truth comes out
I see it in your eyes
I've heard it through others
I didnt want to believe it
Now I can't help it
I can no longer deny
You've been playing a game
You've picked the wrong girl
If you break me apart
You'd wish you hadn't
Trust me when I say
I am not one to be tested

BURN

You can burn in Hell
I do not care
You can let me down
I will rise again
What are you gonna do now?
Now that you've broken me apart
What are you gonna do now?
Now that I'm out of your reach

You Tell Me

You tell me you want me
Then never show
You tell me you need me
Then never call
You tell me you love me
Then don't play along
You tell me you miss me
Then you are never home
You tell me I am the only one
But you are never alone

You tell me never to leave
But you run away
You tell me never to give up
But you are giving in
You tell me not to cry
But you cause me pain
You tell me never to forget
But you have forgotten me
You tell me never doubt your love
But you don't understand

How can I doubt something I have never felt?

Who I Am vs Who I Can Be Part I

I'm very intelligent and wise, yet at times can be so ignorant

I can grow crazy over the littlest things, yet remain calm when it means everything

I know I am far from perfect, but I also know I try far too hard to be

I'm harder on myself than anyone when I've made the tiniest mistake

Inside I care too much what people think, yet I don't give a fuck if you like me or not

When I fall apart or breakdown, it's rare and it means that I honestly care

I'm the most forgiving person I know, yet never forget when someone has stabbed my heart

I can be so beautiful and carefree, yet at times I can be so ugly and jealous

I can be unbearably saddened, yet at times I can be contagiously happy

I'm the sweetest person you'll ever meet, Yet at times I'm a raging bitch

I can be so hard to reach, it's nearly impossible to break through my exterior,

Though once you've reached that place, I'll stay by your side through anything

I'm known to be pathetically emotional when I've drank a little bit too much

I can also be the life of the party, singing and dancing all night long

I'm a very classy girl, yet at times I can act so damn immaturely.

I'll rage and I'll throw punches, then I'll cry and beg you to forgive me

I'm the most trustful person you'll ever know, yet at times I won't trust you

I will turn to ice if you piss me off, but don't you dare ever put me off

I can be paranoid, loud and outspoken or I can be silent, nurturing and loving

I don't take risks until I calculate every consequence that could happen next

Yet at very rare times to be cherished, I will jump right in and risk everything

Who I Am vs Who I Can Be Part II

I am determined and forceful at times, but only when it truly matters to my heart

I'm the kind of girl that wants you every day, yet at times I need to enjoy my own space

I can't stand a spineless weak man, yet need a man who will play by my rules

I'm the most controlling person I know, yet need someone who can put me in my place

I am independent and strong willed, yet when I am in love grow intensely weak

I've been drowned by my own tears, yet still crave the touch of past mistakes

I can be so hardheaded it's insane, but also the most compromising person you'll ever meet

I'm anally clean and a neat freak kind of person, yet for some reason my car is always dirty

I'm not a prissy girl most of the time, yet I always walk with my head held high

I need to know when I'm needed more, but I'll be never overly affectionate towards you

I'm real and I speak my mind, yet there's things you'll never hear and I'll never share

And at times I will run and hide behind the barbed wire walls around my heart

I believe in dreaming, fate, and God, I don't believe in the impossible

I don't give up easily when it matters, but it only takes me one split second to change my mind

To turn around and walk away, and once I do, after all that I will take for you

I will never look back and I will have no regrets, maybe I am just like you

The bottom line is, I am proud of who I am, though not always proud of my actions

But I am after all just a human being, and must keep climbing to reach eternity

Thank You-Epilogue

God gave me the gift of writing, but life (my children, love, family, wonderful times and not so wonderful times, karma, betrayal, shitty ass people, hard learned lessons, mistakes made and so on and so forth) gave me the experiences to inspire my thoughts and emotions. Once I started writing these down, I never stopped.

This book has been thirty years in the making, and I cannot express in words how blessed and emotional I feel to be where I am today and have the opportunity to publish this collection. I write with raw emotion and every word means something to me that can take me back to just a moment in time-whether good or bad.

I cannot thank each and every person that has supported me and is reading this right now, how much it means to me! In life, we all go through so much and sometimes, it is just comforting to know you are not alone.

Without writing, music, my children and God… I do know where I would be today; to be honest. It has been a very long and hard twisting road, but here I am! Don't ever give up on your dreams! If it can happen to me, it can happen to YOU!

With Love,

Rachel

Made in the USA
Monee, IL
03 May 2025